GREECE &
GREEK ISLANDS

Travel Guide Book

A Comprehensive 5-Day Travel Guide to Greece and the
Greek Islands & Unforgettable Greek Travel

◆ *Travel Guides to Europe Series* ◆

Passport to European Travel Guides

❧

Eye on Life Publications

Greece & the Greek Islands Travel Guide Book
Copyright © 2017 Passport to European Travel Guides

ISBN 10: 1548189995
ISBN 13: 978-1548189990

~

Other Travel Guide Books by Passport to European Travel Guides

Santorini, Greece

Top 10 Travel Guide to Italy

Naples & the Amalfi Coast, Italy

Rome, Italy

Venice, Italy

Florence, Italy

Paris, France

Provence & the French Riviera, France

Top 10 Travel Guide to France

London, England

Barcelona, Spain

Amsterdam, Netherlands

Prague, Czech Republic

Berlin, Germany

Munich, Germany

Vienna, Austria

Istanbul, Turkey

Budapest, Hungary

Brussels, Belgium

"Greece is the most magical place on Earth."
–Kylie Bax

Table of Contents

• Map of Greece •

• Introduction •

Greece & the Greek Islands. A highly sought after dream locale hugged by the mesmerizing sapphire waters of Southeastern Europe. It takes only one visit and we're quite certain you'll never want to leave! The historic majesty of its capital city, Athens, the black sand beaches and luminous white buildings with powder-blue dome caps of the myriad Greek islands make for a spellbinding and picturesque temptation to return again and again.

In this 5-day guide to Greece & the Greek Islands, you'll find a variety of our top recommendations and helpful tips to prepare you for having the best travel experience during your time in Greece! Read over the insider tips carefully and familiarize yourself with the information about preparing for your trip. Every traveler has different preferences, and we've included a wide range of recommendations to suit all tastes and budgets.

You're welcome to follow our detailed 5-day itinerary to the letter, or you can mix and match the activities at your own discretion.

Most importantly, we know you're sure to enjoy the beautiful island chain paradise of Greece—and you'll certainly fall in love at first sight with all it waits to offer!

Do enjoy!

The Passport to European Travel Guides Team

• Country Snapshot •

Language: Greek

Capital: Athens

Climate: The climate in Greece is typical of the Mediterranean climate: mild and rainy in the winter months, then relatively warm and dry in the summer, with lots of sunshine throughout most of the year. However, due to the geographical position of Greece and the Greek Islands, there are a number of microclimates here as well.

Borders: Greece shares borders with Albania, Bulgaria, Turkey and Macedonia

Currency: Euro € (EUR)

Country Code: 30

Religion: Eastern Orthodox Christianity

Emergencies: 112 (all emergencies within the European Union), 171 (tourist police), 100 (police), 199 (fire department), 166 (first aid, EMS). The emergency calls at 112 are answered in Greek, English, French, and German.

• Before You Go... •

✔ Have a Passport

If you don't already have one, you'll need to **apply for a passport** in your home country a good two months before you intend to travel, to avoid cutting it too close. **You'll need to find a local passport agency,** complete an application, take fresh photos of yourself, have at least one form of ID and pay an application fee. **If you're in a hurry,** you can usually expedite the application for a 2-3 week turnaround at an additional cost.

✔ Need a Visa?

You can use the following to find out if you need a visa to enter **Greece**:

http://livingingreece.gr/2007/06/10/non-eu-countries-visa-free-travel-to-greece

If you are a **US or Canadian citizen**, you are not required to apply for a visa unless you plan to stay in Greece for **more than 90 days**. European citizens can enter Greece with only a national identity card.

The US State Department provides a wealth of country-specific information for American travelers, including **travel alerts and warnings**, the location of the **US embassy in each country**, and of course, **whether or not you need a visa** to travel there!

http://travel.state.gov/content/passports/english/country.html

✔ Healthcare

Most people neglect this, but it's important to keep in mind when traveling to any foreign country. It's wise to **consult with your doctor** about your travel plans and ensure **routine immunizations are current**. You want to protect against things like influenza, polio, chickenpox, mumps, measles, etc.

If you are a European citizen, a **European Health Insurance Card** (EHIC) covers you for most medical needs, **but not for non-emergencies**. The card is available from health centers and post offices throughout the European Union.

Citizens from other countries should find out if there is **a reciprocal arrangement for free medical care** between their home country and Greece. If you do have **insurance at home**, be sure to check with them about **traveler's coverage**. It's important to know how you'll pay for services in case of an emergency while you're away.

Give your insurance information and passport at the time services are rendered, and **save receipts and bills** so your insurance company can reimburse you if appropriate.

✓ Set the Date

Greece is one of the only locations in Europe with a **desert climate in some locations, such as Santorini**. There are basically two seasons: **April to September** is the **warm, dry season**, and **October to March** is the **cold, rainy season**.

We think the best time to visit Greece is in the fall, when the weather is generally warmer **during the day** and there are better rates and fewer crowds. **Springtime** is beautiful but tends to be chilly on the islands, with windy temperatures that can dip into the 50s.

Most people visit Greece during **the summertime**, so you need to book your hotel **at least two months** in advance if you plan on visiting between **June and August.**

Also note that most hotel **prices double** during the high season. So if you're looking for the best bargains, **wintertime** is your best bet, but expect a lot of rain and chill.

✓ Pack

• We recommend packing **only the essentials** for the season in which you're traveling. By far, the most important thing to pack is a good pair of **walking shoes** (walking boots or light, comfortable sandals and sneakers). Many streets in Greece are made of cobblestone, so good walking shoes are necessary!

• Always **bring an umbrella** whenever you travel. **Unexpected showers** can often ruin a great day of sightseeing.

• **In the colder months**, bring a warm sweater, clothes that you can layer, and a rain jacket. And definitely don't forget **sunscreen, sunglasses, and a hat**.

• **A backpack** can be handy during the day when you go out sightseeing and collecting souvenirs, particularly when getting on and off buses, boats, trams, etc.

• **Travelers from outside Europe** will need to bring along a **universal electrical plug converter** that can work for both lower and higher voltages. This way you'll be able to plug in your cell phones, tablets, curling irons, etc., during the trip.

• **Although English** is spoken around tourist areas, **you'll likely encounter more people who only speak Greek**. So bring a **Greek phrase book** along with you so you can greet appropriately and ask common questions.

• **Hand sanitizer** is always great to have along with you when traveling.

• A simple **first aid kit** is always a good idea to have in your luggage, just in case.

• **Take pictures of your travel documents and your passport** and email them to yourself before your trip. This can help in the unfortunate event they get lost or stolen.

• **Medication.** Don't forget to have enough for the duration of your trip. It's also helpful to have a **note from your physician** in case you're questioned for carrying a certain quantity.

• **Pack lightly**. Getting on and off planes, water taxis and ferries will be very tiring if you have lots of luggage.

✓ Phone Home

How will you call home from Greece? Does your cell phone company offer service while abroad? **What are their rates?**

There are many ways to **call home** from Greece that are inexpensive or completely free.

You may also **sign up for roaming or Internet hotspots** through your own cell phone provider. You can also use Skype, WhatsApp, Viber, or many other voice-over IP providers that are entirely free.

Other options for longer stays are to buy a Greek **phone chip** for your phone (which also gives you a Greek phone number), purchase **calling codes** before you leave home, or you can buy **calling cards** or **prepaid cell phones** once you arrive in Greece.

✓ Currency Exchange

Greece uses the **euro** as its currency (same for most of Western and Central Europe). Check out the **currency exchange** rates prior to your trip. You can do so using the following or many other online currency exchange calculators, or through your bank. For the best rates, we recommend **wait-**

ing until you arrive in Greece to buy euros. http://www.xe.com/currencyconverter

Also, make sure your bank knows you'll be traveling abroad. This way you avoid having foreign country transactions flagged and declined, which can be extremely inconvenient.

✓ Contact Your Embassy

In the unfortunate event you should lose your passport or be victimized while away, **your country's embassy** will be able to help you. Be sure to give your itinerary and contact information to a close **friend or family member**, then contact your embassy with your emergency contact information before you leave.

✓ Your Mail

Ask a neighbor to **check your mailbox** while you're away or visit your local post office and request a hold. **Overflowing mailboxes** are a dead giveaway that no one's home.

• Getting in the Mood •

Here are a few great books and films set in or about Greece & the Greek Islands that we recommend you watch in preparation for your trip to this historic country!

• What to Read

Nikos Kazantzakis is one of the most famous writers who hail from Greece. His great novel _Zorba the Greek_ is a must read for intimate insight into Greek culture. This classic novel is the story of two men, their amazing friendship, and the importance of living this life to the fullest—a fantastic message for your trip to Greece!

• What to Watch

Summer Lovers is a 1982 film starring **Peter Gallagher and Daryl Hannah**, shot on location in

Santorini. Michael (Gallagher) and his childhood sweetheart Cathy (Hannah) travel to Greece to spend the summer in Santorini, where Michael finds himself enchanted by another woman, despite his love for Cathy. He becomes torn between the two, and you won't believe where things go from there — **it's definitely worth a watch!**

A captivating WW2 film, ***Captain Corelli's Mandolin*** (2001), is the love story of an Italian officer and a Greek woman. It is a beautiful movie starting Nicholas Cage and Penelope Cruz and we highly recommend checking it out prior to your trip!

• Local Tourist Information •

As soon as you arrive at the airport, train station or seaport in Greece, you can pick up brochures, city maps, and other helpful information from the regional tourism board. You can also **ask any questions you might have** and rest assured that a friendly, English-speaking attendant will be happy to help.

The local **tourist bureaus** can provide you with information about everything from public and private transportation, to upcoming special events happening countrywide.

Also, most hotels in Greece have maps available for guests as well as a variety of tips about area restaurants, museums, and local seasonal events.

• About the Airports

If you arrive at the **Athens International Airport** (Eleftherios Venizelos), there are a few options for continuing on to the Greek Islands. Either take a nice leisurely ferry or "Flying Dolphin" ride (both from the port in Piraeus or Rafina), or you can fly with a local airline to islands further away, such as Santorini and Crete. **Athens's airport website is:** https://www.aia.gr/en/traveler

Santorini (Thira) National Airport is an airport in Santorini/Thira (JTR), just north of the village of Kamari. It serves as a military and civilian airport.

http://www.hcaa.gr/en/our-airports/kratikos-aerolimenas-santorinhs-kasr

Crete also has a small airport (**Heraklion International Airport**) that you can fly into en route to other Greek islands.

http://www.hcaa.gr/en/our-airports/kratikos-aerolimenas-hrakleioy-n-kazantzakhs

• How Long is the Flight?

To Athens:

• **The flight to Athens from New York City** is approx. 10 hours

• **From London** is approx. 3.5 hours

• **From Hong Kong** is approx. 15 hours

• **From Moscow** is approx. 4 hours

• **From Sydney** is approx. 21.5 hours

• **From Toronto** is approx. 10 hours

• **From Beijing** is approx. 14 hours

• **From Paris** is approx. 3.5 hours

• **From Cape Town** is approx. 16.5 hours

• Overview of Greece
& the Greek Islands •

Greece and its islands wait to charm you with their whitewashed houses, mouth-watering seafood, fascinating ancient history and surprisingly relaxed lifestyle. And don't miss the ancient ruins! Is it any wonder Greece is a country at the heart of any archeological research and scientific endeavor?

This nation, **where democracy was born** in the sixth century B.C., has periodically suffered the unfortunate loss of freedom but never fails to reinvent itself again and again each time.

Athens should be at the top of your itinerary. As the capital and largest city in Greece, it's also the site of the marvelous ancient Acropolis of Athens, a UNESCO World Heritage Site not to be missed during your trip!

It is estimated that Greece has approximately **6,000 islands and islets**. Most are in the Aegean Sea (south and east of the Greek mainland), while a few are in the Ionian Sea (west of the mainland). The largest of these is Crete. And we think the most beautiful and most geologically interesting island is Santorini. Do you agree?

Enjoy Greece!

• Insider Tips For Tourists •

Etiquette

• **Walking Etiquette:** There are very few side-walks in many towns in Greece, so **be careful while walking about narrow**, steep streets and passage-ways. You may need to give way to the occasional speeding scooter, or step aside for a donkey.

• **Dining Etiquette:** Be sure to eat everything on your plate, especially if invited to someone's home. If you know you won't be able to eat everything on your plate, tell the hostess it's too much right away.

• **Body Language Etiquette:** Avoid causing un-intentional offense in Greece with these gestures: 1) Holding your palm out to someone, and 2) Making the "OK" sign: forming a circle with your thumb and forefinger — both gestures are considered to be very rude in the culture.

• **Nodding your head** "yes" or shaking your head "no" may not always be understood in Greece. Locals generally just move their head forward slightly for "yes," and move it slightly backward for "no."

• **Touring Etiquette:** One of Greece's biggest plagues is the abundance of stray dogs—they're everywhere. So beware the dogs and avoid petting or feeding them.

• **Drinking Etiquette:** Greeks like to drink alcohol but they expect decent behavior even while under the influence. The legal drinking age in Greece is eighteen; and sixteen with adult supervision.

As for drinking water in Greece: the water is drinkable in most areas of the mainland, but on the islands, it's best to drink bottled water only. Most of the islands lack a sufficient water supply, so water is imported for every day living—bathing, doing laundry, etc.

Time Zone

Greece is in the Central European Time Zone (UTC + 2). There is a **7-hour time** difference between New York City and Greece (Greece is ahead on the clock). When it is 8:00 a.m. in New York City, it is 3:00 p.m. in Greece).

Saving Time & Money

• **You can spend less on lunch** by buying yummy street food all over the country. **Gyros and souvlakis** are tasty, filling, and inexpensive. You can also snack on **refreshing coconuts** still in their shells, **fresh pastries**, and more!

• **Always double check your bill** in restaurants and ensure the prices reflect the ones on the menu.

• If you're planning to **island-hop**, the cost of taking inter-island ferries and/or water taxis can add up pretty quickly. So we recommend taking the **overnight ferries**—you can save up to 50% off the daytime rates, plus save the cost of the night's stay in a hotel.

• **Planning ahead** is always best when on a budget. If you book the ferries **at least two months in advance**, you can save up to 25% off the cost of your tickets.

• If you visit Greece in the **warmer months**, you can save money by **camping out** instead of booking a hotel or hostel. You may notice that camping in places not designated for it is largely accepted in Greece.

• **Rent a moped** for quick and easy transportation around the island that's less expensive and more convenient than renting a car or taking taxis from place to place. It's also a great way to explore the island's towns and cities more intimately. You can usually rent a moped for under $20 USD per day.

Tipping

Tipping is not mandatory in Greece, although most **taxi drivers** and **some wait staff** will expect it from tourists. **Restaurant bills** will already include a service charge, but if your service is remarkable and you're inspired to leave an additional tip, ask your server if they get to keep their tips before **rounding your bill** up a bit as a thank you, particularly when **paying in cash**; i.e., if your bill is €18.35, you can give €20. (Some restaurants do not allow their servers to keep tips, so whatever you leave will just amount to paying more for the food.)

If you stay in a hotel for more than a couple of nights, it's appropriate to leave a few euros for the **chambermaid**.

When You Have to Go

"Where is the bathroom?" in Greek is: Parakalo, pou ine i tualetta? (Πού είναι η τουαλέτα)

Public toilets in Greece are pretty rare. The ones you do find may not be very clean. The better cafés, bars, restaurants and museums will usually have clean restrooms. You may have to buy a soft drink or small treat to use it in most restaurants and cafés.

Be aware that you generally cannot flush toilet paper down the toilet on many of the islands. The sewage system cannot handle it. Always remember to **throw the toilet paper in the waste bin or bag provided** after use. (There may be a few exceptions in nicer accommodations, but not many.)

Taxes

In Europe, a **Value Added Tax (VAT)** is added to the majority of goods and services and should be incorporated in the advertised price. As of this writing, **VAT in Greece is 23%** for everything except certain items, such as food, books, newspapers and pharmaceuticals, which can range from 6.5%-16%.

If you live outside of Europe, you can be reimbursed for private, non-commercial purchases that included VAT and exceed about $80 USD. **For tourists**, VAT is refunded on purchases taken out of the country.

When you shop in locations bearing a "Tax Free Shopping" or "Tax Refund" logo, ask for a **stamped refund form + your receipt**. You will have up to **five months from the date of purchase** to present the form with your receipts to the custom's office at the airport. The refund can be paid out in cash, as a credit on your credit card, or you can have a check mailed to your home address.

Important to note that items like food, gasoline, alcohol and cigarettes **are not eligible** for a tax refund.

Phone Calls

The **country code** for Greece is 30.

When calling home from Greece, first dial 00. You will then hear a tone. Then dial the country code (1 for the U.S. and Canada, 44 for the UK, 61 for Australia, 7 for Russia, 81 for Japan, and 86 for China), then the area code **without the initial 0**, then the actual phone number.

It can be expensive to call internationally **from a hotel** phone as they assess **heavy surcharges**. Therefore, buying a calling card may be your best bet for staying in touch in a cost-efficient way. There's also Skype, Google Talk, and free texting services like WhatsApp to **stay in touch without cost**.

Electricity

The electrical current in Greece is **220 volts** (for comparison, the US uses 120 volts), with standard European **two-prong plugs**. As previously mentioned, when traveling from outside Europe, you will need to bring an **adapter and converter** that will enable you to plug your electronics and appliances into the wall sockets. Cell phones, tablets and laptop chargers are typically **dual voltage** so you may not need a converter, just an adapter.

In Emergencies

You should keep the following phone numbers handy: 112 (all emergencies), 171 (tourist police), 100 (police), 199 (fire department), 166 (ambulance). The emergency calls at 112 are answered in English, Greek, French, and German. We recommend noting these numbers, writing them down or emailing them to yourself if you have a smart phone.

Greek Phrases For Emergencies:

I am lost	Eho hathi
I need a doctor	Hirazome yiatro
Help!	Voithia!

Call the police!	Fonakste tin astinomia!
Call an ambulance!	Kaleste asthenoforo!
Where is the hospital?	Pou ine to nosokomio!

Pharmacies in Greece are open during **regular business hours** and closed on the weekends. A green cross outside marks the  buildings. Each neighborhood has a 24-hour pharmacy.

Holidays

Every Sunday is a public holiday according to Greek law. **Other national holidays** are as follows:

• January 1 (New Year's Day)
• January 6 (Epiphany)
• February (Clean Monday/Shrove Monday/1st Day of Lent)
• March 25 (Annunciation/Independence Day)
• April (Good Friday/Easter)

• April (Easter Monday)
• May 1 (Labour Day)
• August 15 (Assumption/Dormition of the Holy Virgin)
• October 28 (Ochi Day)
• December 25 (Christmas Day)
• December 26 (Glorifying Mother of God)

Hours of Operation

Museums are generally closed on Mondays and stay open later in the summer months.

Store hours. Keep in mind that **Greek shop owners** siesta (rest) at noon, which can be inconvenient for tourists but it is a well-cherished local tradition.

Don't be surprised if everything's closed. **Many shops and small businesses** close for about **a week in August**, as well as many island hotels from **November until the middle of spring**.

Gas stations are usually open from early in the morning until the evening (approx. 8 or 9:00 pm) and several in each area stay open 24 hours a day. In the islands and the countryside, the gas stations usually take turns in staying open all night, so you will have to check with the locals to find out which gas station is open 24/7 and when.

Money

Greece uses the **euro** (€) as its currency (same for most of Western and Central Europe). The best way to get euros is to wait until you arrive in Greece and use your bankcard at any Greek ATM.

Most Greeks, especially in smaller towns, prefer to do business in **cash only**, so be sure to have some on hand at all times. However, we don't recommend having more than about **€200 in cash** at a time. This will minimize the damages in the unfortunate event your money is lost or stolen.

Most establishments accept credit cards but be mindful of **unnecessary fees,** such as being given the option of having your card charged in dollars vs. euros: **always choose euros**. Paying in dollars will usually cost you more in fees.

Climate and Best Times to Travel

Greece has a **Mediterranean climate**. There are basically two seasons: **April to September** is the **warm, dry season**, and **mid-October to March** is the **chilly, rainy season**.

We think the best time to visit is in the fall, when the weather is nice **during the day** and there are better rates and fewer crowds. **Springtime** is beautiful but tends to be chilly on the islands, with windy temperatures that can dip into the 50s.

Most people visit Greece during the summertime, **June thru August**. Peak season.

Winter months see lots of rain and chill, not ideal for sunning yourself on the beaches, but good for exploring the island and hiking. And don't forget your umbrella!

Transportation

There are usually lots of **taxis and buses** waiting outside the airports, train stations and seaports.

The best means of **getting around on the islands** is by **walking or taking the bus.** Walking is easy and convenient, but a bus is the best way to get from town to town. If you plan to tour multiple islands, we highly recommend hiring **water taxis**.

And again, you can also **hire a scooter, quad bike, or even a donkey** to get around!

Driving

There is no need (or much space) for driving around many of the islands. You will get around mostly on foot, by bus, ferry, scooter or donkey, so renting a car is unnecessary; very few locals actually drive. Parking also becomes an issue in many areas, so **we don't recommend renting a car for shorter stays.**

However, in the event you should decide to **rent a car while in Athens**, please ensure you know all **motor vehicle regulations** and laws for driving in Greece. European driver's licenses are accepted for car rentals, but if you're not from Europe, be sure to get an **international driver's permit** before arriving in Greece:

http://www.dmv.org/international-driver-permits.php

• Tours •

These are our **top recommendations** for touring Greece and the Greek Islands, helping you hone in on the very best options available, in our experienced opinion. Be sure to check websites or call for current rates and times. Enjoy!

By Bike

Crete is a cyclist's paradise. We recommend taking a cycling tour of the island with **Backroads** and savoring the amazing views, taste the delicious and fresh seafood and soak up the amazing Greek sunshine!

Location Information:

Backroads
Phone: 800-462-2848 or local: +1 510-527-1555
Website: http://www.backroads.com

Cycle Greece offers some really great cycling tours and their itineraries change all the time, so make sure to consult them by phone (they have an office in New York City and in Athens) or via their website. Some of our favorite Cycle Greece tours are: Cycle Cyclades, Corinthia, Sacred Sites, Crete, and the day trips to nearby Turkey!

Location Information:

Cycle Greece
Phone: New York: 800-867-1753 Athens: +30 210-921-8160
Website: http://www.cyclegreece.gr

By Boat

Don't miss this awesome **Viator day cruise from Athens**, visiting the nearby beautiful islands of **Poros, Hydra and Aegina!** A coach will scoop you up from your hotel or a central meeting location, then you'll be taken to the port of Piraeus to board your ship. What a wonderful day!

Location Information:

Viator — Hydra, Poros and Aegina Day Cruise From Athens
Phone: (888) 651-9785
Website: https://www.viator.com

Dakoutros Bros J.V. (**Santorini Excursions**) offers a great boat tour of the volcano! It's inexpensive and runs about three hours. You want to book this tour well in advance. And for more romantic experiences, the sunset excursion they offer will be perfect!

Location Information:

Santorini Excursions (Dakoutros Bros J.V.)
Address: Firá Central Square, Santorini
Phone: +30 228 602 2958
Website: http://www.santorini-excursions.com

We think **Crete** offers some of the very best boating experiences in Greece and have two top recommendations!

See beautiful Chania with **Captain Nick's Aphrodite Boat Trip in Chania!** You'll have a marvelous time snorkeling and swimming with Captain Nick and his awesome team.

Location Information:

Tour of Chania by Captain Nick's Chania
Phone: +30 282 108 6732
Website: http://www.captainnickchania.com

We also love **Cretan Daily Cruises**! They offer fantastic daylong boat trips departing from the seaside town of Kissamos to Imeri Gramvousa Island and Balos Lagoon. The trip offers time on the exotic beaches of ancient and archeological sites (Venetian castle), and a relaxing time aboard the ship.

Location Information:

Cretan Daily Cruises
Phone: +30 282 202 2888 or +30 282 202 4344
Website: http://www.cretandailycruises.com

By Bus

Dolphin Hellas has a wonderful site for finding the perfect couch tours from Athens! Professional guides accompany you in very comfortable coach buses. For overnight tours, hotel accommodations are included.

Location Information:

Dolphin Hellas Travel & Tourism
Phone: +30 210 922 7772

Website: http://www.dolphin-hellas.gr

While in Athens, step into ancient Greece with Greeka.com's amazing **Hop On Hop Off** bus tour! The buses start running at 9:00 a.m. but you can hop on at any of the many stops along the 90-minute route through historic Athens. Visit many attractions, including the Temple of Zeus, the Acropolis, the bustling Plaka and the New Acropolis Museum, just to name a few. Enjoy!

Location Information:

Greeka.com
Phone: +30 21850 3006
Website: http://www.greeka.com

Key Tours offers a wonderfully immersive exploration of **Santorini** in just one, fun-filled day! Visit the Monastery of the Prophet Elias, have your Kodak moments in the lovely village of Pyrgos, then hop a couple boats to visit the legendary volcano!

Location Information:

Private Tours Greece
Phone: +30 210 923 3166
Website: http://www.keytours.gr

Try Special Interest or Walking Tours

Wine Tasting and Corinth Shared Bus Tour is a fabulous specialty day tour from **Athens Tours Greece!** You'll spend about 8 hours seeing some phenomenal sites along the way, including: the Temple of Apollo, the Corinth Canal, Nemea, the beautiful Greek countryside and famous wine vineyards—and of course, enjoy plenty of wine!

Location Information:

Athens Tours Greece: Wine Tasting and Corinth Bus Tour
Phone: +30 210 451 6106
Website: http://www.athenstourgreece.com

Viator offers a delectable 3.5-hour **food tour of Thessaloniki**, the culinary capital of Greece! You'll start off with a nice, strong cup of Greek coffee, then tour great gastronomic highlights that include: visiting the central marketplace, specialty shops, fun eateries and street food! Enjoy strolling along the Aegian Sea, and, at the end, relaxing in a local tavern.

Location Information:

Viator: Thessaloniki Food Tour
Phone: (888) 651-9785
Website: http://www.viator.com

And if you're an **ancient history buff**, or simply want to tour with true experts, we highly recommend any one of **Andante Travels'** edifying multi-day Greek tours! From the Peloponnesian hillside and the birthplace of the Olympics, to the rich Minoan history in Santorini and Crete, to the debate grounds of Socrates and other well-revered philosophers, Andante's definitely got you covered!

Location Information:

Andante Travels (Experts in Archeological Travel)
Phone: (888) 331-3476
Website: https://www.andantetravels.com

Booking a nice **hiking trail tour** from the town of Firá to Oia in beautiful Santorini might be just the thing you need. We love it! This **Viator** tour takes you to all the places you need to see in the areas without getting lost in the narrow, complicated pathways around the island. Bring your camera and be prepared for astonishing views of Santorini!

Location Information:

Viator — Private Tour: Santorini Sightseeing Firá to Oia Hiking Trail
Phone: (888) 651-9785
Website: http://www.viator.com

• 5 Days in Greece & the Greek Islands •

Enjoy this 5-day itinerary for a well-balanced and enjoyable experience! Be sure to check websites or call for current rates and times. You can follow this itinerary to the letter, or you can modify and adjust for time, interest and/or preferences. Either way, we're sure you'll have great fun!

• Day 1 •

When you arrive in Athens and get checked into your hotel accommodations (hopefully you arrive in the morning or early afternoon), have a short rest, get refreshed and renewed, then head out to the **Acropolis** and see the **Parthenon**. See if you can figure out how it was built in the fifth century! Then venture around the famed **Plaka** village, happily perched in the shadow of the grand Acropolis.

If you don't make it out to the islands, spending time in the Plaka can make up for it. Pop into the various **shops, cafés and restaurants**. You'll find plenty of tourist shops with gorgeous postcards, trinkets and souvenirs for ferrying home. The handmade jewelry shops have a special place in our hearts! Some pieces are most enchanting.

Don't miss the museums. Among them are the Folk Art Museum, the Children's Museum, the Jewish Museum and the Music Museum.

For lunch in the Plaka, we recommend **Vyzantino Restaurant**. This is a venue frequented by locals, not just tourists, which means you'll get a much more authentic taste of Greece.

For dinner this evening, why not treat yourself to a fine dining experience at Spondi's?

Location Information:

Acropolis of Athens
Address: Athens, 105 58, Greece
Website: http://www.acropolisofathens.gr

Vyzantino Taverna-Estiatorio Restaurant
Address: 18 Kidathinaion Str., Plaka, Athens
Phone: +30 210 322 7368

Website: http://www.vyzantinorestaurant.gr

Spondi Restaurant
Address: 5 Pirronos | Pagkrati, Athens
Phone: +30 210 756 4021
Website: http://www.spondi.gr

• Day 2 •

We think your **second day** in Athens is perfect for a day cruise! Book **Viator's wonderful tour** of the nearby islands, **Hydra, Poros and Aegina** for today and enjoy!

Location Information:

Viator — Hydra, Poros and Aegina Day Cruise From Athens
Phone: (888) 651-9785
Website: https://www.viator.com

• Day 3 •

Today let's head off to Santorini! No trip to Greece is complete without visiting this world-famous locale. Yes, tourism abounds, but Santorini, Mykonos and Crete are three of the must-see islands when visiting Greece — so if you have more than five days to spend, please do island hop!

You have a couple of options for getting to Santorini from Athens, you can take a ferry or a 45 minute flight. If you choose the ferry, you can go fast or slow. **The slower**, less expensive option costs about 40 euros and takes about eight hours. **The faster** option runs about 75 euros and takes about five hours.

If you're only in Athens for five days, we highly recommend the faster option or flying, to afford yourself more time in Santorini. You can check **Let's Ferry** for scheduling. If you choose to fly, **Ryanair** airlines usually has the least expensive flights from Athens to Santorini, sometimes as low as $40-$50 USD.

If it isn't raining and the sun's nice and bright, you can **head to the beach** when you arrive and get settled in your hotel!

Santorini has some of the most beautiful and unique **beaches** in the world. Most are covered with volcanic black sand. The most popular beaches are: **Perivolos**, on the island's south end; **Kamari**, which is about six miles southeast of the town of Firá and features gorgeous views of the shining rock at night; **Red Beach**, which is smaller and more crowded, but is arguably one of the most famous and beautiful beaches in all of Santorini; **Vlychada**, a long gray sand covered beach with sun lounges for relaxing after a long day on the water; and **Perissa**, a black sand paradise about nine miles from Firá on the island's southeast end.

Plan to spend at least half a day at the beach—and don't forget your sunscreen!

Another option is to visit one of Santorini's many **wineries.** You can book the **Santorini Wine Adventure Tour!** Our top recommendation for wine enthusiasts.

Alternatively, you can go **horseback riding**! Ride around Santorini's hills or along the shores of the marvelous beaches. Riding is a great afternoon or evening activity and you can even choose to ride on a donkey! Check out **Aegean Wonder—Santorini Tours!**

After a long day of traveling and **getting a taste** of being in one of the world's most sought after vacation spots, head back to your hotel and **rest up** for tomorrow!

Location Information:

Santorini Wine Adventure Tours
Address: Firá, Santorini
Phone: +30 693 296 0062 or +30 228 603 4123
Website: http://www.winetoursantorini.com

Aegean Wonder — Santorini Tours
Address: Fira, Santorini
Phone: +30 698 059 3626
Website:
http://awsantorinitours.com/horseback-riding.html

• Day 4 •

Our top recommendation for seeing the island today is **My Santorini's** *See Santorini in One Day* bus and boat tour! It leaves at around 9:00 a.m. and returns about a half-hour after sunset. It's truly a magnificent experience! They take you to the most magical panoramic views of the island, and experienced tour guides regale you with the area's rich, thought-provoking history.

It makes for a most memorable day in Greece!

Location Information:

My Santorini (Pelican Travel Services)
Address: Firá, Santorini
Phone: +30 228 602 2220
Website: http://www.mysantorini.com

• Day 5 •

If this is your last day in Greece, you'll likely be heading back to Athens to catch an evening flight. **If time permits**, spend some time exploring the port town of **Piraeus** before you go. Just seven miles outside of Athens in the Attica region, Piraeus is one of the most important ports in the Mediterranean. Life centers around three main port areas: the central port, Mikrolimano, and the Bay of Zea marina.

The Zea marina has lots of great **restaurants, bars, taverns and shopping prospects** for choice souvenirs. Another great place for shopping would be Monastiraki of Piraeus, a great market for bargainers.

And try not to miss **Kastella**, a popular and beautiful quarter of Piraeus built on a hill, also known as Prophet Ilias. If you walk to the top, you'll see alleys of picturesque houses. **The outdoor theatre here, Veakio**, hosts many incredible cultural events in the summer months.

If you're in Greece for **more than five days**, we hope you're off to **Mykonos or Crete** today! Plenty of ferries to these islands from Santorini, about three hours to Mykonos and two to Crete on the faster boats.

We would also recommend those with longer stays head up to **Thessaloniki**, the second largest city in Greece, after the first couple of days touring Athens.

Enjoy!

• **Best Places For Travelers on a Budget** •

Best Bargain Sleeps

Metropolis Hotel in **Athens** is a good, inexpensive option for accommodations in the capital. Located two blocks from Syntagma Square, and within walking distance of the Plaka, this hotel offers great views of the Acropolis and a central location for good rates!

Location Information:

Metropolis Hotel
Address: 46 Mitropoleos Str., Athens, Greece
Phone: +30 211 198 5351
Website: http://www.hotelmetropolis.gr

Pella Hotel is also a great option for inexpensive accommodations in Greece, in the wonderful city of **Thessaloniki!** Pella is just a few steps from the famed Egnatia Street and offers great rooms for the price.

Location Information:

Pella Hotel
Address: 63 Ionos Dragoumi St., Thessaloniki
Phone: +30 231 052 4221
Website: http://www.pella-hotel.gr

If you are looking for an inexpensive spot while in beautiful **Santorini**, **Villa Manos** is the way to go. A charming, family run hotel in the heart of the island, you'll be hard pressed to find a better value!

Location Information:

Villa Manos
Address: Karterados, Fira, Santorini
Phone: +30 228 602 2882
Website: http://www.villamanos.gr

If you're visiting **Mykonos** on a budget, we highly recommend the **Aeolos Hotel**! Perfect location for sightseeing and shopping, large and comfortable rooms with a very friendly staff. An excellent value!

Location Information:

Aeolos Mykonos Hotel
Address: Argirena, Mykonos Town, Mykonos
Phone: +30 228 907 8033

Website: http://aeolos-hotel.com

On Crete, the best value in our opinion can be found at the quaint **Renieris Hotel**. Family-owned and charmingly hospitable, you might never want to leave this spotless hotel! The location is central to many of Crete's top attractions and we consider the room views an attraction unto themselves. Enjoy!

Location Information:

Renieris Hotel
Address: 1 Psathi Hill, Stalos, Crete
Phone: +30 282 106 8763
Website: http://renierishotel.gr

If you head for a stay in **Delphi**, **Hotel Galaxidi** is our favorite option. Charming atmosphere, we love their breakfast, gorgeous views from the balconies, and the hospitality is first rate for the price.

Location Information:

Hotel Galaxidi
Address: 11 Andrea Siggrou | Town Center, Galaxidi, Greece
Phone: +30 226 504 1850
Website: http://www.hotelgalaxidi.gr

Best Bargain Eats

In Athens we love and highly recommend **Bairaktaris!** Juicy souvlaki, delicious pitas, gyros, kebabs, salads, you name it! It's here for an inexpensive price; also centrally located near many attractions. Don't miss it!

Location Information:

Bairaktaris
Address: 2 Plaka Monastirakiou, Athens, Greece
Phone: +30 210 321 3036

Palati Restaurant is a great option for inexpensive dining in **Thessaloniki**. The restaurant is located in the old Egyptian market. You can also listen to live music (at just the right volume!) while enjoying your tasty meal.

Location Information:

Palati Restaurant
Address: 3 Ladadika Platia Morihovou, Thessaloniki
Phone: +30 231 055 0888
Website: http://www.palati.gr

In **Delphi**, head over to **Telescope Café**. Very nice ambiance and delicious food and wines at very reasonable prices.

Location Information:

Telescope Café
Address: 31 Vassileon Pavlou & Friderikis, Delphi
Phone: +30 226 508 3123

The **Good Heart** is a great spot in **Santorini** that won't break the bank. A family-run tavern, The Good Heart has scrumptious views and serves delicious and authentic Greek cuisine made with fresh ingredients and a homemade flair.

Location Information:

The Good Heart
Address: Faros Street, Akrotiri, Santorini
Phone: +30 228 608 2247

Kikis Tavern is our favorite spot when budgeting in **Mykonos**. It's very popular so there may be a bit of a wait, but the food and value are well worth it!

Location Information:

Kikis Tavern
Address: Agios Sostis Beach, Mykonos
Website:
https://www.facebook.com/pages/Kikis/10640
0416113933

Head over to **Erganos** in **Crete**. Frequented by locals, the traditional Greek fair is tasty and the music makes you feel right at home. You can make reservations.

Location Information:

Erganos Tavern
Address: Georgiadi 5, Heraklion, Crete
Phone: +30 285 629 2810
Website: http://www.erganos.gr

• Best Places For Ultimate Luxury •

Best Luxury Sleeps

Hotel Grande Bretagne is our top luxury recommendation when staying in **Athens**. This historic hotel is a landmark in the heart of the city that offers great rooms, and an amazing rooftop restaurant.

Location Information:

Hotel Grande Bretagne
Address: 1 Vasileos Georgiou A' str., Syntagma Square, Athens, Greece
Phone: +30 210 333 0000
Website: http://www.grandebretagne.gr

And you can always stay in historic **Thessaloni-ki** and look no further than the elegant **Grand Hotel Palace**! This chic, cosmopolitan hotel simply oozes the best in luxury and pampering. You'll look forward to returning after enjoying a day of sightseeing and never want to leave.

Location Information:

Grand Hotel Palace
Address: 305-307 Monastiriou str., Thessaloniki
Phone: +30 231 054 9000
Website: http://grandhotelpalace.gr

One of the most luxurious and beautiful hotels in **Santorini** is the **Canaves Oia Hotel**. Located on one of the highest points of the island, Canaves Oia offers stunning views and opulent guest rooms. Next to the main hotel are the beautiful Canaves Oia Suites and Canaves Oia Villas. Both suites and villas offer stunning accommodations and privacy for large families or for more intimate getaways.

Location Information:

Canaves Oia Hotel
Address: Oia 84702, Santorini
Phone: +30 228 607 1453 or +30 228 607 1427
Website: http://canaves.com

If you choose to include **Delphi** on your itinerary, we highly recommend the lovely **Aegli Arachova Hotel**! In the nearby mountain village of Arachova, we love the hypnotic scenery and elegant suites.

Location Information:

Aegli Arachova Luxury Hotel
Address: Eparchiaki odos Arachovas-Eptalofou, Arachova, Greece
Phone: +30 226 703 1767 or +30 226 703 1761
Website: http://www.aegli-arachova.gr

To pamper yourself in **Mykonos**, we simply *must* send you to the **Myconian Ambassador Hotel**! You will likely need a taxi to and from the city center, but the location, service and lavishness make it well worth it nonetheless. It's also perfect for romantic getaways!

Location Information:

Myconian Ambassador Hotel
Address: Platis Gialos, Mykonos
Phone: +30 228 902 4166
Website: http://www.myconianambassador.gr

Daios Cove is a fabulous luxury resort hotel on **Crete** if you decide to spend the night on the island. It's an amazing five star beach resort with spectacular amenities, villas and great food — our favorite accommodation on the island!

Location Information:

Daios Cove Luxury Resort & Villas
Address: Vathi Beach, Agios Nikolaos, Crete
Phone: +30 284 120 0488
Website: http://www.daioscovecrete.com

Best Luxury Eats

Spondi Restaurant in **Athens** is a ritzy, vibrant restaurant serving contemporary Mediterranean cuisine. Spondi's is located in the heart of Athens and features a vaulted stone dining room & gorgeous courtyard. The food and drinks are delicious, of course, and not your typical Greek fare — they come with a nice twist.

Location Information:

Spondi Restaurant
Address: 5 Pirronos | Pagkrati, Athens
Phone: +30 210 756 4021
Website: http://www.spondi.gr

In Thessaloniki, Kritikos Gallery & Restaurants offers the best in fine dining in the area. We love the excellent ambiance, presentation and sumptuous Mediterranean flavors.

Location Information:

Kritikos Gallery & Restaurants
Address: 5B Venizelou Street, Panorama, Thessaloniki
Phone: +30 231 033 2810
Website: http://www.okritikos.com

Epikouros Taverna in **Delphi** is a great restaurant to visit if you end up in this part of Greece. It offers great traditional Greek dishes with a tiny twist in each and the views of the valley from your table will be quite stunning!

Location Information:

Epikouros Taverna-Restaurant
Address: 33, Vas. Pavlou & Freiderikis str, Delphi
Phone: +30 226 508 3250

Website: http://www.epikouros.net

Ambrosia Restaurant in Oia, **Santorini** is a must if you visit the island! It offers one of the most beautiful terrace views in all of Greece (there are two terraces to choose from) and the food is beyond delicious. Ambrosia is perfect for intimate candlelight dinners. Reservations are a must and can be hard to come by, so be sure to book well in advance of your trip.

Location Information:

Ambrosia Restaurant
Address: Cliffside Terrace at Village Center, Oia, Santorini
Phone: +30 228 607 1413
Website: http://www.restaurant-ambrosia.com

On Mykonos, high-end dining doesn't get any better than **Narcissus Mykonos**. A true culinary gem located in the Kouros Hotel, the wine selection and savory local dishes are first-rate!

Location Information:

Narcissus Mykonos
Address: Kouros Hotel | Mykonos, 846 00
Phone: +30 228 902 5381
Website: http://www.kouroshotelmykonos.gr

For the best gourmet dining on **Crete**, book a reservation at the **Blue Monkey Asian Restaurant**, a magical dining experience in the Amirandes Luxury Resort. They serve such delicious Asian cuisine — we think you may end up dining here more than once!

Location Information:

Blue Monkey Asian Restaurant
Address: Amirandes Grecotel Resort | Crete
Phone: +30 289 704 1103
Website: http://www.amirandes.com

• Greek Nightlife •

Best Bars in Greece & the Greek Islands

Brettos Bar in the heart of **Athens** is cozy and understated, definitely worth a visit to experience authentic Greece. Almost always full, Brettos is a charming local staple that's been around since 1909. They make their own liquors in more than 30 delicious flavors!

Location Information:

Brettos Bar
Address: 41 Kidathineon, Athens
Phone: +30 210 323 2110
Website: http://www.brettosplaka.com

Tango Bar is the place to check out in **Thessaloniki.** A well-known and lively nightlife locale, you'll no doubt enjoy a night of great live music and dancing among the locals, as Tango's calendar of events is always full!

Location Information:

Tango Bar
Address: 19 Diam. Olympiou, Thessaloniki
Phone: +30 694 585 2307

Casablanca Soul Bar is a great spot in **Santorini** for a good time. Located on the rim of the volcanic caldera of downtown Firá, it's one of the hottest spots for nightlife in Santorini. Popular bands from around the world are invited to perform live at the Casablanca. It's great fun after a day out in Firá!

Location Information:

Casablanca Soul Bar
Address: 12 Ypapantis, Firá Downtown
Phone: +30 697 757 5191
Website: http://casablancasoul.com

The happening spot in Mykonos is definitely the **180° Sunset Bar!** Great music enhanced by hypnotic views of the Aegean Sea with exotic drinks available for good measure. You may just be out until the wee hours of the morning!

Location Information:

180° Sunset Bar
Address: 25 Iordani | Panigiraki, Mykonos Town
Phone: +30 699 360 1424

Our top recommendation on Crete is **Eclipse Bar Platanias**! Open from April to October, they throw the absolute best parties on the island in our humble opinion, hands down. If you're visiting when they're in season, don't miss it!

Location Information:

Eclipse Bar Platanias
Address: Eclipse Bar Platanias | Khania, Greece
Phone: +30 282 106 8139
Website: http://www.eclipseplatanias.com

Best Clubs in Greece & the Greek Islands

Pixi Club is another spot we highly recommend for **a great night out**. Situated in the lively nightlife district of Gazi, Pixi's a fully renovated, upscale industrial space in the center of **Athens**, filled with music, 3D projections, and electric music. You'll likely be out pretty late!

Location Information:

Pixi Club Athens
Address: 11 Evmolpidon St., Athens
Phone: +30 210 342 3751
Website: http://www.pixi.gr

Enzzo De Cuba is a great place to visit if you are looking for a great club near **Athens**. The club is considered an all-time classic, a standard meeting point since the 90s for clubbers in the Attica area.

Location Information:

Enzzo de Cuba
Address: 72 Agias Paraskevis, Peristeri, Greece
Phone: +30 210 578 2610
Website: http://www.enzzodecuba.gr

And if you are looking for a great nightclub in **Thessaloniki, Block 33** is our favorite spot! It's a happening venue for live music, dancing and great drinks.

Location Information:

Block 33
Address: 26is Oktovriou 33, Thessaloniki, Greece
Phone: +30 231 053 3533
Website: http://www.block33.gr

Enigma is a great, three-room club we like a lot in **Santorini**. It's almost legendary on the island for modern disco and great drinks. Frequented by a range of age groups, everyone can have a good time at Enigma.

Location Information:

Enigma Club
Address: Thíra, Kikladhes, Santorini
Phone: +30 228 602 2466
Website: http://enigmaclub.gr

Paradise Club is the happening spot when in **Mykonos**. Arguably the best nightclub on the island, this club offers a fantastic night out on the town with mesmerizing views, attentive staff and awesome house music. You're in Mykonos, baby!

Location Information:

Paradise Club
Address: Paradise Beach, Cyclades Islands, Mykonos
Phone: +30 694 946 8227
Website:
http://www.paradiseclubmykonos.com

If you want to party the night away in **Crete**, head out to the sophisticated **SixtySix Disco Lounge**

Bar. Give the DJ a special request and lose your-self in Crete's intoxicating nightlife — right here!

Location Information:

SixtySix Disco Louge Bar
Address: 66 Andrea Papandreou, Elounda, Crete
Phone: +30 284 104 2002

Best Live Music in Greece & the Greek Islands

Hands down, the Half Note Jazz Club is our top recommendation for the best live music in **Athens!** Top musicians from all over the world perform here so check the calendar and the night out!

Location Information:

Half Note Jazz Club
Address: 17 Trivonianou, Athens
Phone: +30 210 921 3310
Website: http://www.halfnote.gr

Tango Bar has the best live performances in **Thessaloniki.** A well-known and lively nightlife locale, you'll no doubt enjoy a night of great live music and dancing among the locals. Tango's events calendar is always full!

Location Information:

Tango Bar
Address: 19 Diam. Olympiou, Thessaloniki
Phone: +30 694 585 2307

Our favorite live performance spot in Greece is **Greek Nights at Dimitris Restaurant** in **Santorini!** Especially great on hot summer nights, this spot offers great food and wonderful live entertainment. Local dancers and musicians will amaze you with traditional Greek music and dance.

Location Information:

Dimitris Restaurant
Address: Kamari, Santorini 84700
Phone: +30 693 247 5154
Website: http://santorinidimitris.com

Sky Lounge on Kamari Beach is another fabulous **Santorini** spot for great live music and a good time. It's a cozy restaurant/bar and live music venue with a modern décor. Good drinks and snacks are served.

Location Information:

Sky Lounge
Address: Kamari Beach, Kamari, Santorini
Phone: +30 693 941 8960
Website: http://www.santorini-skylounge.com

Don't miss the sunset parties at **Scorpios** in **Mykonos**! The musical vibes reach right into your soul. Truly a highlight of this magical island.

Location Information:

Scorpios Mykonos
Address: Paraga, Mykonos
Phone: +30 228 902 9250
Website: http://www.scorpiosmykonos.com

Best Theatre in Greece & the Greek Islands

Since **Athens** is a city known for its many theatres, you should definitely visit the **National Theatre of Greece** while you're in town. Opened in 1880, it's considered one of the best venues and it's our top recommendation.

Location Information:

National Theatre of Greece
Address: 22-24 Agiou Konstantinou St., Athens
Phone: +30 210 528 8100
Website: http://www.n-t.gr/en

Another choice spot for a night at the theatre is the **National Theatre of Northern Greece** in **Thessaloniki**. It's not just a place to see theatrical performances, but also fascinating concerts, festivals and art exhibitions.

Location Information:

National Theatre of Northern Greece
Address: 2 Ethnikis Amynis Str., Thessaloniki
Phone: +30 231 520 0000
Website: http://www.ntng.gr

The White Door Theatro in Firá is a great interactive dinner theater where you're sure to have a great night in **Santorini!** Traditional Greek fare like olives, cheese, salads and bread are included in the entrance charge.

Location Information:

The White Door Theatro
Address: Fira, 84700, Santorini
Phone: +30 228 602 1770
Website: http://www.whitedoorsantorini.com

• Conclusion •

The **Greek peninsula** is at the crossroads of three continents: Europe, Africa and Asia, and is bordered by the Aegean, Ionian, and Mediterranean Seas. It's an absolutely marvelous locale for an unforgettable vacation!

We hope you enjoyed reading our guide to **Greece and the Greek Islands**, and found great tips and recommendations for discovering some of Greece's uniquely rich history, architecture, arts, beaches, food, music and the many other attractions this great country has on offer!

Warmest regards,

The Passport to European Travel Guides Team

Visit our Blog! Grab more of our signature guides for all your travel needs!

http://www.passporttoeuropeantravelguides.blogspot.com

★ **Join our mailing list** ★ to follow our Travel Guide Series. You'll be automatically entered for a chance to win a **$100 Visa Gift Card** in our monthly drawings! Be sure to respond to the confirmation e-mail to complete the subscription.

• About the Authors •

PASSPORT TO
European Travel
The Best Travel Guides to Europe!

Passport to European Travel Guides is an eclectic team of international jet setters who know exactly what travelers and tourists want in a cut-to-the-chase, comprehensive travel guide that suits a wide range of budgets.

Our growing collection of distinguished European travel guides is guaranteed to give first-hand insight to each locale, complete with day-to-day, guided itineraries you won't want to miss!

We want our brand to be your official Passport to European Travel — one you can always count on!

Bon Voyage!

The Passport to European Travel Guides Team

http://www.passporttoeuropeantravelguides.blogspot.com